Garden Furniture

JOHN BOWLER

MINI · WORKBOOK · SERIES

MURDOCH BOOKS®

CONTENTS

Making outdoor furniture   4

Fold-up table and chair   6

Barbecue table and bench   16

Circular seat   24

Adjustable lounger   30

Swing seat   38

Arbour seat   46

Traditional garden chair   54

Tools for making garden furniture   63

Index   64

Swing seat (top left) and barbecue table and bench (bottom left)

Making outdoor furniture

Building outdoor furniture requires the same skills and tools as any other carpentry job, and as always a little forward planning will make the work much easier. Careful choice of materials will also result in a beautiful and long-lasting piece.

SUITING YOUR GARDEN

Before you begin work, spend some time deciding exactly what sort of garden furniture you need. Do you need a table for food or drinks as well as seats? Is your garden very small so that folding furniture is most suitable? Do you want furniture that is easily moved around the garden?

There is nothing worse than having your garden full of beautiful furniture you never use, so plan your requirements carefully.

CHOOSING MATERIALS

Outdoor furniture is, by its very nature, subjected to the weather and the materials you use must be able to withstand the elements if the item is to remain in good condition.

Suitable timbers include treated pine, Western red cedar and iroko. The latter two are much more expensive than pine, but can be worth the expense as they are very attractive. All timbers used outdoors require a protective finish, and the finish you choose will also affect your choice of timber. For instance, using iroko would be a waste if you are planning to paint the item, but if you are planning to use a clear oil finish

to achieve a natural look, it might be worth the expense.

The nails, screws and bolts you use for outdoor furniture should always be galvanised so that they don't rust.

WORK AREA

• A specific workshop area isn't a necessity for building any of the projects in this book. However, some pieces are quite large and you will need space to store materials and to

Treated pine was used for this setting as it was to receive a painted finish.

have enough space to move easily around the project during the construction. An undercover area such as a garage might suffice, but if you don't have a fixed roof to work under, make sure you can keep the timber dry and clear of the ground while it is stored.

• Good lighting is a necessity, not only for comfort, but for safety. Fluorescent lights are the best choice because they cast a brighter light with less shadow. Take care where you position your lights so you are not working in your own shadow and the light isn't in your eyes.

• Adhesives and paints can give off dangerous fumes, so always work in a well-ventilated area. Open windows and doors when applying adhesives or finishing coats.

• While an old table may be strong enough to serve as a workbench for small items, you will need a strong bench for most of these projects.

EQUIPMENT

Most of these projects can be completed using basic hand tools, but portable power tools will make the job easier and faster. A circular saw, electric drill, jigsaw and router are the most commonly used power tools in the home workshop.

SAFETY PRECAUTIONS

When using any type of portable power tool, make sure you are wearing the right safety gear. Always wear safety glasses that completely enclose the eyes and a dust mask (the

Outdoor furniture such as this arbour seat turns a garden into living space.

cartridge type is recommended if you have any respiratory problems). If you have long hair, tying it back is not enough protection – a cap or hairnet is essential. Also consider what clothing you will wear. Loose-fitting garments are dangerous when working with machinery.

BEFORE YOU START

Read right through the entire instructions before you begin a project. Check that you have the right tools, timber and hardware specified. If you are not familiar with a particular technique then try practising on a scrap of timber.

There when you need them, folded away out of sight when you don't, this table and chair are made from dressed hardwood and then given a colourful finish with a gloss paint designed for exterior use.

Fold-up table and chair

This table and chair are simply made with slats glued and nailed to the rails. For ease of folding the chair seat swivels on steel rods; the table legs are held in place against a timber block.

MAKING THE TABLE TOP

1 Cut two side rails to length. Square a line 10 mm in from each end around the rail. Round the ends with abrasive paper to the set-out line.

2 Cut sixteen slats 450 mm long. Use abrasive paper to round the top edges of the slats along both sides and ends. Measure in 6 mm from each end of the slats and square a pencil line across the face edges.

3 Stand the rails on edge and about 350 mm apart. Apply PVA adhesive along the top edge of one rail. Place one slat at a 90 degree angle across the rails, lining up the outside edge with the 10 mm line on the glued rail. The slat should overhang the rails by 6 mm on each side (use the squared line as your guide).

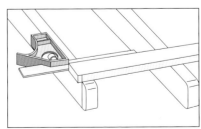

3 Place the slat at 90 degrees to the rails, lining up the outside edge with the 10 mm set-out line.

TOOLS

- Tape measure and pencil
- Tenon saw
- Power mitre saw
- Jigsaw
- Cork sanding block
- Try square
- Builders square
- Hammer and nail punch
- Set square 60/30
- Vice or cramps
- Screwdriver
- Electric drill
- Drill bits: 3 mm, 4.5 mm, 6 mm, 8 mm countersunk
- Adjustable spanner
- Marking gauge
- Router
- Router bit: 8 mm straight
- Bevel
- Chisel: 25 mm
- Sawhorses (optional)

4 Fix the slat to the rail with two 25 x 2 mm panel pins. Place the second slat at the other end and fix it in the same manner. Apply PVA adhesive to the other rail and nail the slats in place, taking care to keep the

MATERIALS★

PART	MATERIAL	FINISHED LENGTH	NO.
Table			
Inside leg	30 x 18 mm hardwood	630 mm	2
Outside leg	30 x 18 mm hardwood	610 mm	2
Side rail	40 x 18 mm hardwood	465 mm	2
Slat	25 x 13 mm hardwood	450 mm	16
Stretcher rail	18 x 18 mm hardwood	268 mm	2
Stop block	18 x 18 mm hardwood	265 mm	1
Chair			
Front leg·	65 x 18 mm hardwood	900 mm	2
Back leg	25 x 18 mm hardwood	605 mm	2
Side rail	40 x 18 mm hardwood	420 mm	2
Back rail	40 x 18 mm hardwood	370 mm	1
Front rail	30 x 25 mm hardwood	370 mm	1
Seat slat	25 x 13 mm hardwood	370 mm	15
Back slat	65 x 13 mm hardwood	480 mm	2
Front stretcher rail	30 x 13 mm hardwood	480 mm	1
Back stretcher rail	30 x 13 mm hardwood	455 mm	1

OTHER: Abrasive paper: 80 grit and 120 grit; PVA adhesive. *For table:* 25 x 2 mm panel pins; four 65 mm x 8 gauge countersunk screws; two 40 mm x 8 gauge countersunk screws; two 25 mm x 8 gauge countersunk screws; two 45 x 6 mm machine bolts; two dome nuts; washers. *For chair:* four 40 mm x 8 gauge countersunk screws; twelve 25 mm x 8 gauge screws; two 50 x 6 mm countersunk machine bolts with dome nuts and washers to suit; 25 x 1.5 mm panel pins; 388 mm length 8mm plain steel rod; 450 mm length 8 mm threaded steel rod with 20 mm thread each end or fully threaded; dome nuts and washers to fit rod; finish of choice

★ All materials quoted are planed measurements. Finished size: table 400 mm wide x 465 mm deep x 510 mm high; chair 480 mm wide x 500 mm deep x 840 mm high.

overhang in line and the rails and slats parallel. Position the remaining slats on the rails and fix with a 3.5 mm gap between each slat. A spare nail makes a handy spacer to keep the gaps between the slats even.

ADDING THE LEGS

5 On the bottom of each leg use a set square to mark a 60 degree angle on the face (see the diagram on page 10). Square a line down each face edge. Clamp the leg on a firm surface and cut the angle with a tenon saw. On the inside legs, measure 615 mm from the bottom on the longest side. Mark a 60 degree angle parallel to the first and cut it. Mark the centre across the width (see diagram detail A on page 10), place a try square on the end and mark a 90 degree angle across the face from the centre. Continue the line down the edge and end. Cut with a tenon saw.

6 Cut the two outside legs 610 mm long, measured along the longest side, and square the top. Measure 15 mm from the top; drill a 6 mm hole through the centre. Round off the top with abrasive paper. Measure 320 mm from the bottom along the longest edge on all four legs and drill a 4.5 mm hole through the centre.

7 Cut a pair of stretcher rails 268 mm long. On each end of one spreader rail, mark diagonals across the ends and then drill a 3 mm pilot hole in the centre.

8 Place the outside and inside legs together, with the 60 degree angles facing one way on the inside legs and in the opposite direction on the outside legs. Screw a 65 mm x 8 gauge countersunk screw through one pair of legs into the pilot hole at the end of the stretcher. Place a washer under the screw head and between each part. Turn the screw enough to hold the legs together but still allow movement. Repeat for the other side.

9 The other stretcher is fixed at the top of the inside legs. Drill a 4.5 mm hole through the leg 10 mm from the top. Line up the rail with the angle on top of one leg and drill a 3 mm pilot hole through the leg into the end of the rail. Countersink the top of the hole if desired. Apply a little PVA adhesive to the end of the rail and fix it with a 40 mm x 8 gauge screw. Just across from the screw, drive a 25 x 2 mm panel pin through the leg into the rail. This will prevent the rail turning. Repeat on the other side.

ASSEMBLING THE TABLE

10 With the table top upside down on a firm surface, measure 70 mm from the end of one side rail and square a line across the edge and side of the rail (see the side rail detail on page 10). Measure 20 mm from the lower edge and drill a

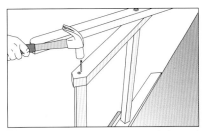

9 Line up the square corner of the rail with the bevel on top of the inside leg and fix it in place.

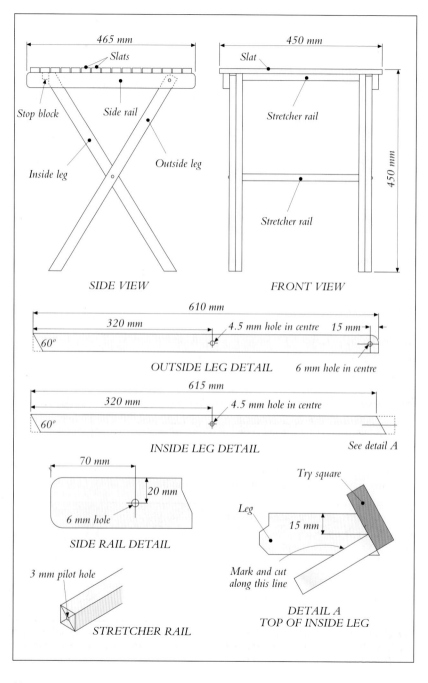

465 mm

Slats

Stop block

Side rail

Inside leg

Outside leg

SIDE VIEW

450 mm

Slat

Stretcher rail

Stretcher rail

450 mm

FRONT VIEW

610 mm

320 mm

4.5 mm hole in centre   15 mm

60°

OUTSIDE LEG DETAIL   6 mm hole in centre

615 mm

320 mm

4.5 mm hole in centre

60°

INSIDE LEG DETAIL   See detail A

70 mm

20 mm

6 mm hole

SIDE RAIL DETAIL

3 mm pilot hole

STRETCHER RAIL

Try square

Leg

15 mm

Mark and cut
along this line

DETAIL A
TOP OF INSIDE LEG

6 mm hole through the rail. Repeat on the other rail.

11 Cut a stop block 265 mm long. Drill a 4.5 mm hole through it, 25 mm from each end. Centre the block between the rails underneath the second slat. Screw in place with 25 mm x 8 gauge screws.

12 Stand the legs within the rails. Place a washer between the leg and rail. Insert the 45 x 6 mm machine bolts through the outside leg and out through the side rail. Secure with a dome nut and washer.

13 Check the action of the folding legs and adjust as required. Turn the table right way up and check that the top is level. If not, adjust the stop block. Sand and apply the finishing coat of your choice.

MAKING THE CHAIR LEGS

14 Cut two front legs to length. Measure 150 mm from one end (top) and square a line across the face (see front leg detail on page 12). Set a marking gauge to 40 mm and mark from the squared line down the length of the leg.

15 At the top end, mark 40 mm from the opposite edge. Select a thin piece of timber (ply is ideal) and bend it from this mark to the 150 mm line on the edge. Trace the curve onto the leg with a pencil. Mark a pencil line 40 mm parallel to this curve, lining up with the gauged line. Clamp the leg firmly to the bench or sawhorses so the curve overhangs the end. Cut the curves on the waste side with a jigsaw. Smooth the curve with 80 grit abrasive paper. Mark and cut a 60 degree angle on the bottom of the leg. Repeat for the other leg.

16 Cut two back legs to length. Measure 180 mm from the bottom and then a further 230 mm (see back leg detail on page 12). Square these two marks across the face of the leg. Position one leg in a vice (or clamp it to sawhorses) so that both square marks are on the same side and are kept clear of the vice jaws. Make certain the face is above the surface of the bench.

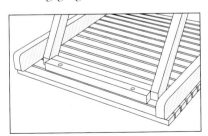

11 Centre the stop block between the rails underneath the second slat and fix it in place with 25 mm screws.

15 Bend a thin piece of timber between the 40 mm and 150 mm marks to make the curve for the back.

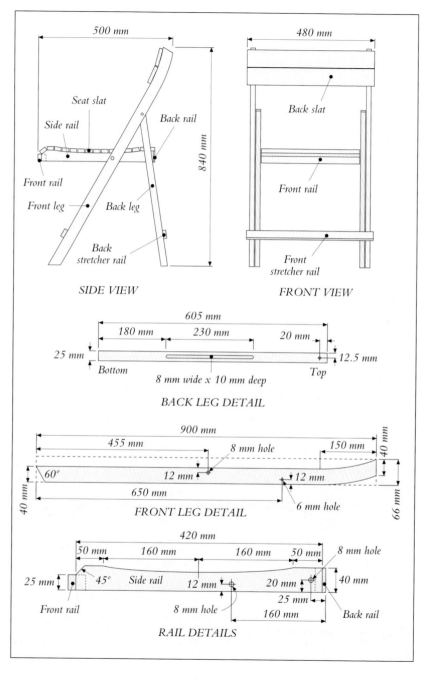

500 mm

Seat slat

Side rail

Back rail

840 mm

Front rail

Front leg   Back leg

Back
stretcher rail

SIDE VIEW

480 mm

Back slat

Front rail

Front
stretcher rail

FRONT VIEW

605 mm

180 mm   230 mm   20 mm

25 mm   12.5 mm

Bottom   Top

8 mm wide x 10 mm deep

BACK LEG DETAIL

900 mm

455 mm   8 mm hole   150 mm   40 mm

60°   12 mm   12 mm

40 mm   650 mm   66 mm

6 mm hole

FRONT LEG DETAIL

420 mm

50 mm   160 mm   160 mm   50 mm   8 mm hole

25 mm   45°   Side rail   12 mm   20 mm   40 mm

Front rail   8 mm hole   25 mm   Back rail
160 mm

RAIL DETAILS

17 Set up a router with an 8 mm straight cutter to cut 10 mm deep. Fasten the guide fence to the router at 8 mm from the edge of the cutter. Test on a piece of scrap 25 x 18 mm timber and check the set-up. The cut should be in the centre of the timber. Hold the router up from the surface of the leg between the set-out lines, with the guide fence against the side. Start the router and slowly lower the cutter onto the leg. Machine the groove along the leg, taking care to stop at the squared set-out lines. Repeat the process on the other leg. Round each end of the legs slightly with abrasive paper.

MAKING THE SEAT

18 Cut the side rails to length. Measure 50 mm from each end and square a line across the face. Mark the centre point between the lines (160 mm) and square another line across the timber. To produce the curved seat, measure 10 mm from the top edge of the side rail and tack in a small nail, leaving the head standing up around 15 mm. Bend a thin piece of timber around the nail to line up

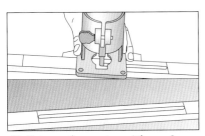

17 Set up the router with an 8 mm straight cutter to cut 10 mm deep. Centre the cut between the set-out lines.

on the top edge with the squared lines. Trace the curve with a pencil. Hold the rail firmly in a vice or cramp, remove the nail and cut the curve on the waste side of the line with a jigsaw. Smooth with abrasive paper. Use the first rail as a template to cut the other rail. At the front ends of the side rails measure 25 mm from the bottom edge and cut off the top corner at 45 degrees.

19 Cut a back rail to length. Measure in from each end the thickness of the side rail (18 mm) and square the line across the face and down each side. Then set a gauge to 12 mm and, working from the face, mark from the squared line across the end and down the other. Hold the rail face up in a vice or cramp and cut the shoulder to the gauge line. With a 25 mm chisel, remove the bulk of the waste by chiselling down the grain. Clean and level the bottom of the joint by chiselling across the grain of the timber.

20 Cut the front rail to length. In either end cut rebates 18 mm wide and 12 mm deep for the side rails in the same way as in the back rail.

21 Place one side rail in the rebates in back and front rails and drill a 4.5 mm clearance hole through the side rail, approximately 10 mm in from each end. Countersink the holes if required. Drill a 3 mm pilot hole into the back and front rails. The hole at the back is drilled at a slight angle

to ensure the screw goes into the rail, but not at too much of an angle or it will go out the side. Repeat for the other side rail. Apply PVA adhesive to the rebate joints and screw the frame together with 40 mm x 8 gauge screws.

22 Cut fifteen seat slats to length. Round the top edges and ends with abrasive paper. Apply adhesive to the 45 degree angle on the side rails. Place the first slat on the angle so it rests against the front rail. Nail through the face into the side rail with 25 x 1.5 mm panel pins. Glue and nail the second slat so it touches the first. Glue and nail the remaining slats, using a 2.5 mm nail as a spacer. Check the slats lie parallel and adjust if required. Sand the outside edges flush with the rail and slightly round over the top edge.

ADDING THE BACK SLATS

23 The back slats are attached to the top of the front legs. Cut the two slats to length and slightly round over the edges with abrasive paper. Measure 25 mm in from each end

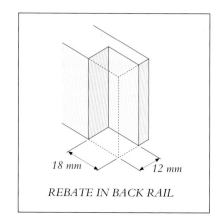

18 mm   12 mm

REBATE IN BACK RAIL

and approximately 12 mm from each edge and drill two 4.5 mm clearance holes. Countersink the top of the hole. Place a slat on one front leg, 20 mm down from the top with a 12 mm overhang on the outside. Line up the holes with the centre of the leg. Drill 3 mm pilot holes into the leg and fix with 25 mm x 8 gauge screws. Use a builders square to ensure the job is square. Fix the second slat parallel to the first with the same overhang. Place the two slats over the opposite leg. The gap between the legs must be 415 mm. Screw-fix as before.

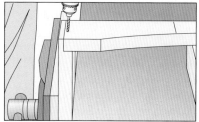

21 When fixing the back rail, angle the screw slightly to ensure it goes into the rail.

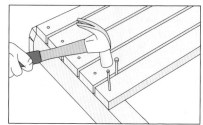

22 Use a 2.5 mm nail as a spacer between the seat slats to ensure the gaps are even.

24 Cut the front stretcher rail to length. Drill a hole approximately 25 mm in from each end and fix it 150 mm from the bottom of the front legs with a 25 mm x 8 gauge screw into each leg as before. Sand and slightly round over the top.

ASSEMBLING THE CHAIR

25 Measure up 455 mm from the bottom of each front leg and square a line across the outside face. To fit the threaded rod, drill an 8 mm hole, 12 mm in from the front edge. In each side rail drill another hole 160 mm from the back and 12 mm up from the bottom edge.

26 Drill another 8 mm hole 25 mm in from the back of the side rail and 20 mm up from the bottom edge for the plain rod.

27 To fix the back legs to the front legs, drill a 6 mm hole through the front leg 650 mm up from the bottom and 12 mm in from the back edge. Measure 20 mm from the top of the back leg and drill a 6 mm hole in the centre. Countersink this hole on the inside (grooved) face. Place a washer between one front and one back leg and thread a 50 x 6 mm machine bolt through. Fix with a dome nut and washer on the outside. Do not fix the other legs yet.

28 Position the seat frame against the joined legs and push the 8 mm plain rod through the seat into the groove in the back leg. Fit the other back leg

The shaped side rails of the chair allow the seat to be curved for comfortable seating.

so the rod is in the groove. Fix the top of this back leg to the other front leg with a machine bolt as before. Insert the threaded rod through the front leg, the seat frame and the opposite front leg. Fit a dome nut on each side.

29 Measure 100 mm up from the bottom of the back legs. Open out the chair so the seat is flat and fix one end of the back spreader rail with a 25 mm x 8 gauge screw, allowing a 12 mm overhang. Check the legs are parallel and then fix the other side to the opposite leg.

FINISHING

30 Check the seat folds smoothly. Adjust it, if necessary, by tightening or loosening the screws.

31 Sand the chair and apply a protective finishing coat of paint.

Barbecue table and bench

This sturdy outdoor setting is simple to make. The construction requires the minimum number of joints and is suitable for the less experienced woodworker.

MAKING THE TABLE TOP

1 Cut two side rails and two end rails to length, using a power mitre saw.

2 Cut a 20 x 20 mm rebate along one edge of each end rail using a router. Measure in 70 mm from each end and square a line across the rebated side and edge. Set a marking gauge to 20 mm (the width of the rebate), turn over the rail and, working from the rebated edge, mark a line from the end to the 70 mm line. This part will be removed to create a flat section for the dowelled joint. Use a tenon saw to cut across the rebate and then a jigsaw to cut along the line. Round over the edge with abrasive paper.

3 Mark the dowel set-out on each end of the side rails (see the diagram at right). Use a 10 mm dowelling bit in an electric drill and bore the holes 26 mm deep. Place dowel centres in the holes and position the end rails at right angles to the side rails to mark the corresponding holes. Drill these holes 26 mm deep. Place adhesive in the holes and on the end of the rails. Insert the dowels and place the frame in sash cramps. Use scrap timber between cramps and frame to protect

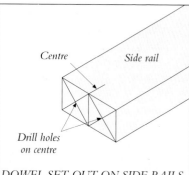

Centre *Side rail*

Drill holes on centre

DOWEL SET-OUT ON SIDE RAILS

A blue-on-white distressed finish gives this bench and table combo a contemporary look. It's perfect for dining al fresco with friends and family.

MATERIALS★

Part	Material	Finished length	No.
Table			
Side rail	70 x 35 mm treated pine	1360 mm	2
End rail	90 x 35 mm treated pine	900 mm	2
Slat	70 x 20 mm treated pine	1360 mm	11
Cleat	70 x 35 mm treated pine	760 mm	3
Stretcher rail	70 x 35 mm treated pine	600 mm	2
Brace	70 x 35 mm treated pine	600 mm	2
Leg	70 x 35 mm treated pine	730 mm	4
Bench			
Leg	70 x 35 mm treated pine	580 mm	4
Bearer	70 x 35 mm treated pine	450 mm	2
Back upright	70 x 35 mm treated pine	630 mm	2
Arm	70 x 35 mm treated pine	550 mm	2
Back slat (top)	90 x 20 mm treated pine	1350 mm	1
Back slat	70 x 20 mm treated pine	1350 mm	2
Seat slat	70 x 20 mm treated pine	1350 mm	1
Seat slat (front)	70 x 20 mm treated pine	1330 mm	5
Stiffener	70 x 35 mm treated pine	1260 mm	1
Rail	40 x 20 mm treated pine	450 mm	1
Cleat	25 x 25 mm treated pine	450 mm	2

OTHER: Epoxy adhesive; abrasive paper: two sheets of 120 grit; eight 50 mm long 10 mm diameter timber dowels; 30 mm x 8 gauge galvanised countersunk screws; 40 mm x 8 gauge galvanised countersunk screws; 50 mm x 8 gauge galvanised countersunk screws; 65 mm x 8 gauge galvanised countersunk screws; 50 x 2.5 mm galvanised decking nails; preservative; finish of choice

★ Finished size: table 1500 mm long x 900 mm wide x 750 mm high; bench 1400 mm wide x 600 mm deep x 840 mm high.

the surface. Tighten the cramps and remove excess adhesive. Measure the diagonals for square. Leave to dry.

4 Cut eleven 1360 mm long slats and round over the ends and edges on the top surface with 120 grit abrasive

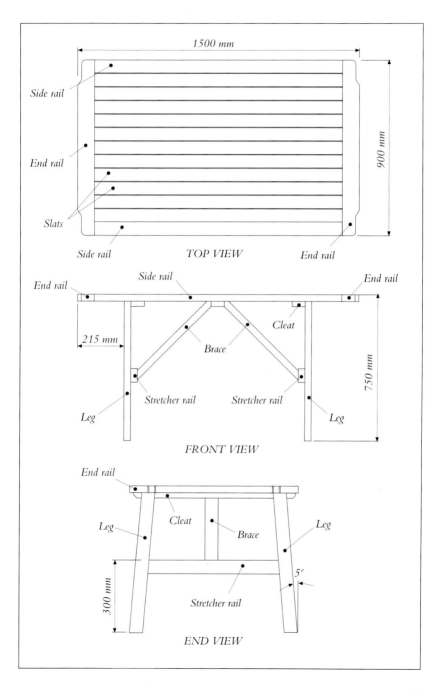

1500 mm

900 mm

Side rail

End rail

Slats

Side rail

TOP VIEW

End rail

End rail

Side rail

End rail

215 mm

Cleat

Brace

750 mm

Stretcher rail

Stretcher rail

Leg

Leg

FRONT VIEW

End rail

Cleat

Leg

Brace

Leg

300 mm

5°

Stretcher rail

END VIEW

paper. Lay the slats out upside down and fit the frame over the slats, allowing a gap of 3–5 mm between each board (a nail placed between the boards makes a useful spacer). For each slat drill one or two 4.5 mm clearance holes through the end rail, then 3 mm pilot holes into the underside of the slats. Hold each slat in position and fix from beneath with 30 mm x 8 gauge countersunk screws.

5 Using the end rail diagram to the right as a guide, make a cardboard template to shape each end rail. Draw the shape onto the rails in pencil. Cut the shape with a jigsaw. Clean the edge and round over with 120 grit abrasive paper.

6 Turn the top upside down and measure in 250 mm from each end. Square this mark across the bottom of the slats. Cut two 70 x 35 mm cleats to fit between the side rails. Bevel-cut the ends to 15 mm thick; round the edges over. Position the cleats on the inside of the marked lines and drill a 4.5 mm clearance hole followed by a 3 mm pilot hole

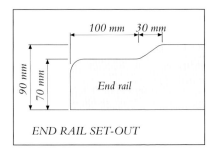

END RAIL SET-OUT

into each slat. Screw the cleats to each slat with a 40 mm x 8 gauge countersunk screw. Fix a third cleat across the centre of the slats. Skew a 50 mm galvanised screw into the side rails from each side of the cleats.

ADDING THE TABLE LEGS

7 The legs are cut with a 5 degree parallel bevel on each end. Set the angle on a mitre saw; or you can set a sliding bevel or create a pitch board (see the diagram opposite). To minimise waste, cut the legs from one length of timber. Bevel-cut one end at 5 degrees. Measure 730 mm, mark and cut parallel to the first cut. Mark and cut the other legs. The angle on the waste side is the same angle required for the next leg.

8 Cut two stretcher rails 600 mm long with 5 degree bevels (angled in opposite directions, not parallel as for the legs) at each end. Measure up 300 mm from the bottom of each leg and square a line across the outside edge. Place the legs flat with the spreader rail on top. Line up the top edge of the rail with the squared lines. Keep the ends flush with the outside edge

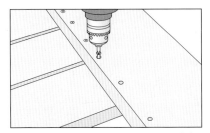

4 Fit the frame over the slats and fix in place with two 30 mm x 8 gauge countersunk screws into each slat.

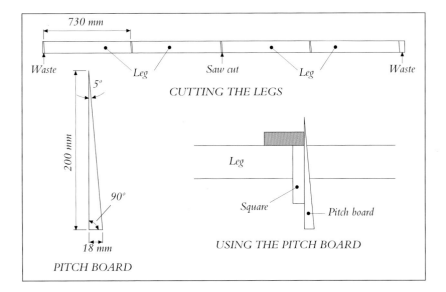

730 mm

Waste   Leg   Saw cut   Leg   Waste

CUTTING THE LEGS

5°

200 mm

90°

18 mm

PITCH BOARD

Leg

Square

Pitch board

USING THE PITCH BOARD

of the legs. Fix in position with two 50 mm x 8 gauge countersunk screws on each leg. Use the pitch board or sliding bevel to ensure the rail is at the correct angle.

9 Stand the assembled leg frame upside down against the outside edge of an end cleat. Centre it against the cleat. Fix each leg with two 65 mm x 8 gauge screws into the edge of the cleat. Repeat at the other end for the other leg frame.

10 To stabilise the table, cut a brace for each leg. Measure from the lower edge of the stretcher rail to the centre cleat. Cut two braces to this length. Fix them with two 50 mm x 8 gauge screws into the centre of the cleat and to the stretcher. Turn the table right side up and lightly sand with 120 grit abrasive paper.

CUTTING BENCH PIECES
11 Cut the four legs 580 mm long. Bevel both ends of each at 5 degrees. Cut two bearers 450 mm long.

12 Cut an 80 degree angle on one end of each bearer. Measure and mark 70 mm in from the opposite end of the bearer and square a line across the top edge (see the diagram on page 22). Square a second line across the same end 10 mm down from

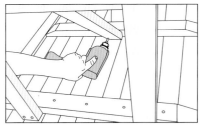

10 To stabilise the table, fix a brace from the lower edge of each stretcher to the centre cleat under the table top.

the top. Join these points on the face and cut the bevel. On the lower edge cut a 45 degree bevel. Cut two 630 mm back uprights, bevelling the top of each as for the bearers.

13 The arms fit around the back uprights and sit on top of the legs. Square-cut one end of an arm. Measure 70 mm from the end and, with a square and pencil, mark a line from the inside edge across the face.

14 Place a bearer on the edge of the arm and use it as a template to mark an 80 degree angle. Square the bevelled mark across the bottom of the arm. Use a gauge to mark 35 mm from the line to the squared end on each face. Remove this corner with a saw by cutting on the waste side of the line. Make the second arm in the same way, but so you have one left and one right arm. Round the ends of the arms with abrasive paper.

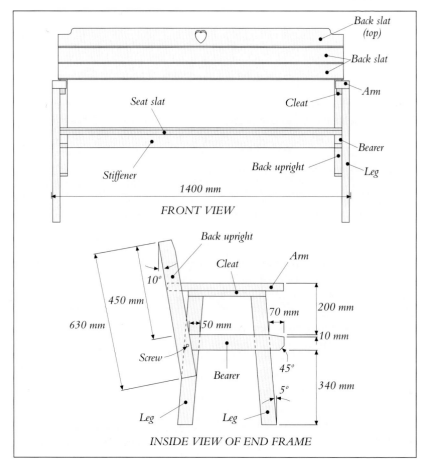

FRONT VIEW

INSIDE VIEW OF END FRAME

15 Cut the back slats. Shape the ends of the top slat with a jigsaw to match the table top. Round the edges with abrasive paper. Cut a design in the centre of the top slat.

ASSEMBLING THE BENCH

16 Square a line 10 mm in from both ends across the back of the back slats. Position the top slat on the bevelled end of one back upright. Line up the squared line with the outside face of the upright and fix with adhesive and two decking nails. Check for square with a builders square. Fix the other end of the slat to the other upright. Nail the other two back slats in place with a 10 mm overhang and a 4 mm gap between each. Cut two cleats from offcuts, turn the frame over and fix them across the back of the slats, 10 mm from the top (see the photograph on page 17).

17 Cut the seat slats. The long slat goes at the front and overhangs the bearers 10 mm each end; the others sit flush on the bearers. Fix them in place as for the back slats. Turn the seat over and cut the stiffener. It fits between the bearers, in line with the second slat. Fix it through the bearers with two 65 mm x 8 gauge screws at each end. Fix a 40 x 20 mm rail across the centre of the slats.

18 Measure up 340 mm from the bottom of each leg on the inside face and mark a line across the face of the leg, parallel to the end. Position each leg against the bearer, lining up the

This simply constructed bench is given an individual touch with a cut-out design in the top slat.

set-out with the bottom edge. The front legs sit against the edge of the front slat. The back legs are fixed 50 mm in from the bevelled end (see diagram opposite) and secured with two 50 mm x 8 gauge screws.

19 The back is positioned so its top is 450 mm above the top of the bearer. Hold the upright against the end of the bearer and fix it in place with two 50 mm screws into the leg.

20 Cut two 450 mm cleats to fit against the inside of the legs at the top. Cut the ends at a 5 degree angle to match the outside of the legs. Fix in place, flush on top and ends, with two 50 mm screws into each leg.

21 Place the arm on top of the legs, against the back. Fix with 50 mm screws through the upright and cleat. Sand the bench and apply a finish to match the table.

You can follow the sun or the shade all day with this clever seating arrangement constructed in treated pine and finished with paint designed for exterior use.

Circular seat

This circular seat is made in eight separate sections that can be joined to surround a tree trunk or other garden feature. Four sections make a semicircle that can stand against a wall.

CONSTRUCTING THE FRAME

1 Cut sixteen front legs and sixteen back legs to length. Use a power mitre saw to ensure an accurate square cut. Measure 70 mm from the top of each front leg and square a line across the face and down each edge. Set the marking gauge to 17.5 mm and mark across the end and down each edge to the 70 mm mark to indicate the halving joint.

2 Place a front leg next to a back leg with the bottom ends flush. Transfer the set-out lines from the front leg onto the back leg to mark a corresponding joint. Mark a cross on the face between the set-out lines. Square the set-out lines across both edges and mark a depth of 17.5 mm between the lines. Repeat for the remaining legs. Adjust the depth of cut on the circular saw to 17.5 mm. Clamp each leg in turn on a set of sawhorses and cut the joints with the saw by lining up the notch in the base plate with the set-out line and cutting on the waste side. Place several intermediate cuts in the timber to help remove the waste. Chisel the waste from each joint, first removing the bulk of the timber by

TOOLS

- Tape or rule and pencil
- Handsaw
- Circular saw
- Power mitre saw
- Jigsaw
- Builders square
- Combination square
- Marking gauge
- Chisel: 25 mm
- Hammer
- Nail punch
- Electric drill
- Drill bit: 4.5 mm
- Screwdriver
- Sliding bevel
- Hand plane
- Sawhorses

striking the chisel with a hammer or mallet, leaving approximately 3 mm of timber in the bottom of each joint. Clean the joint by paring in from each side down to the gauge line. Use the square to check the bottom is flat and adjust if required.

3 Cut the side rails to length. To cut the halving joints, measure 70 mm from each end and square a line

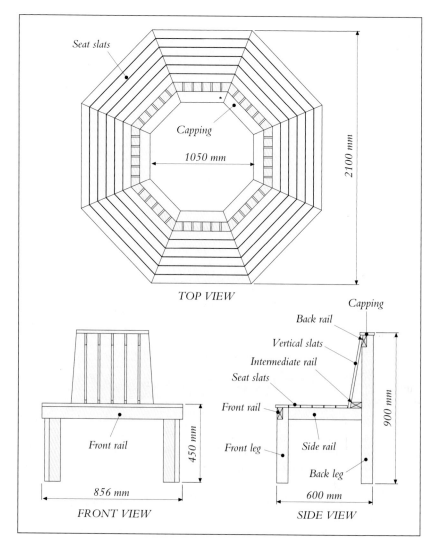

Seat slats

Capping

1050 mm

2100 mm

TOP VIEW

Capping

Back rail

Vertical slats

Intermediate rail

Seat slats

Front rail

Front leg

Side rail

Back leg

900 mm

450 mm

Front rail

856 mm

FRONT VIEW

600 mm

SIDE VIEW

across the face and down each side. Gauge the depth (17.5 mm); cut and remove the waste as before. Check each joint for accuracy of fit.

4 Place one front and one back leg on a flat surface with the recesses face up. Apply preservative to each joint. Place a side rail in the recesses; check the inside of the frame for square. Drill two 4.5 mm holes 20 mm across from the inside of the front joint with 3 mm pilot holes into the leg and secure with 30 mm x 8 gauge

MATERIALS★

Part	Material	Finished length	No.
Front leg	70 x 35 mm treated pine	450 mm	16
Back leg	70 x 35 mm treated pine	875 mm	16
Side rail	70 x 35 mm treated pine	600 mm	16
Back rail	70 x 35 mm treated pine	462 mm	8
Front rail	70 x 35 mm treated pine	856 mm	8
Intermediate rail	70 x 35 mm treated pine	520 mm	8
Vertical slat (side)	90 x 20 mm treated pine★★	450 mm	16
Vertical slat (intermediate)	70 x 20 mm treated pine★★	450 mm	32
Seat slat	70 x 20 mm treated pine★★	870 mm	48
Capping	90 x 20 mm treated pine	480 mm	8

OTHER: 40 x 2.5 mm galvanised twisted-shank decking nails; 30 mm x 8 gauge countersunk galvanised chipboard screws; 50 mm x 8 gauge countersunk galvanised chipboard screws; abrasive paper: 100 grit; preservative; finish

★ Finished size: 2100 mm diameter x 900 mm high.
★★ The seat and vertical slats are cut from treated pine decking.

galvanised chipboard screws through the rail into the leg. In the back leg place a screw 20 mm in from the front edge and the other 20 mm from the back edge. Check the frame for square. The side with screw heads will be the inside of the frame. Assemble the other legs and side rails, so that each seat section will have a left and right frame.

5 Cut the rails to length. To make housings for the front and back rails, measure 70 mm from the top of each leg and square a line across both faces and the front edge. Measure 35 mm from the front edge on the inside face and gauge a line from the top of the leg to the squared lines. Set a sliding bevel to 22.5 degrees and mark a line on the top of each front leg (see the diagram on page 28). Hold the frame upright in a vice and cut down the line on the waste side with a handsaw. Rotate the frame

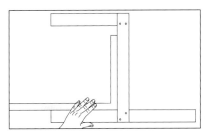

4 Place one front leg, one back leg and one side rail on a flat surface. Check that the frame is square.

90 degrees and cut the shoulders down to the first cut. Check for accuracy of fit and adjust as required.

6 The face of the back rail is bevelled to fit the vertical slats. Gauge a line 12 mm from the face along the top edge of the rail. Set the circular saw to cut at 10 degrees and use a rip fence to ensure a straight cut. Hold the timber firmly on edge in a vice and rip along the gauged line. Stand the rail on edge and cut the ends at 22.5 degrees using a power mitre saw. Apply a coat of preservative to the housings in the back legs and fix the rail flush on the outside face with two 50 mm x 8 gauge galvanised chipboard screws into the leg. The front rail is cut 856 mm long and is fixed in the same manner.

7 The intermediate rail will need one edge to be bevelled to allow the back to be sloped. Gauge a line 12 mm from the front edge along the face. Tilt the circular saw to 10 degrees and set the rip fence to 58 mm. Hold the rail firm in a vice or skew-nail it on a sawhorse. Cut

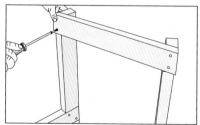

6 Fit the back rail with the bevelled edge on the outside face. Fix it with two screws into each leg.

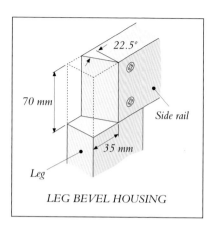

70 mm

22.5°

Side rail

35 mm

Leg

LEG BEVEL HOUSING

the bevel along the length. Place the rail flat on the mitre saw and cut the ends at 22.5 degrees so they finish flush on the ends. Place them against the back legs and drill two holes at each end into the top of each side rail. Fix with 50 mm x 8 gauge galvanised chipboard screws.

ADDING THE SLATS
8 Cut the 90 x 20 mm vertical slats for the back. Position each slat over a side frame. Place a builders square on the top rail and square up the slat so that the outside edge is flush with the end of the intermediate rail. With a pencil, mark the back of the vertical slat, the end and top edge of the top rail. Remove the slat and place it face down on the sawhorses. Mark a line along the length of the slat between these two points. Set your circular saw to 22.5 degrees. Hold the slats firm and rip along the line on the waste side. Ensure that the saw cut bevels the correct way. Remember, the set-out line is on the back of the

slat, therefore the face is wider. You will require one left-hand and one right-hand slat for each section. Stand the slat on edge and cut the top of the marked length with a 10 degree bevel. Use a hand plane to round the edge on the front corner of the bevelled side. Apply some preservative to the rail and to the back of the slat. Fix the slat with two 40 x 2.5 mm twisted-shank nails.

The individual sections are screwed together to form a complete circle.

9 Cut the remaining vertical slats to length with a 10 degree angle on top. Leave a gap of 10 mm between the slats. Fix as for the side slats.

10 The seat slats reduce in length from front to back. Select a straight slat to be cut for a starter board at the front of the seat. Cut one end at 22.5 degrees on the mitre saw. Position this slat with the bevelled end flush with the outside face of the frame. Allow 10 mm to overhang the front rail and mark the length on the underside at the opposite end frame. Turn the board over and cut to this set-out using the drop saw. Apply preservative, then fix the rail with two twisted-shank nails. As you are nailing close to the end, drill a pilot hole to prevent the timber splitting.

11 Cut one end of the next board. Position it on the seat, flush on the angled end. Use a 3 mm nail as a spacer between the boards at each end and mark the underside to determine the length. Cut and fix as for the starter board, ensuring the

ends are flush with the outside of the end frames. Fix the remaining slats in the same way.

FINISHING

12 Apply a finish to each section of the project. If necessary, level the ground around the tree so the seat sits level and all sections line up with each other. Position each section in turn, joining them with 50 mm screws. Fix two screws into the front legs and three into the back legs, keeping the seat and backs aligned.

13 Cut the ends of the capping pieces at 22.5 degrees so that the shorter side fits on top of the back leg. Fix them with decking nails.

13 Cut the ends of the capping pieces at 22.5 degrees and fix them over the top of the back legs.

Adjustable lounger

The cross rails of this elegant lounger are housed into the side rails and the slats are set on edge for extra strength. The back adjusts to three different heights or can be laid flat.

SIDE RAIL HOUSINGS

1 Cut two side rails. Watch for any bows in the timber and keep them facing up. Measure 200 mm from each end and square a line across the face. Measure in 30 mm from these lines and square another line for the foot and head rail housings.

2 At the foot end square the shoulder lines across both the bottom and top face edges. Set a gauge to 10 mm and mark a line between the set-out lines on both edges to indicate the through housing.

3 Set the circular saw for a 10 mm cut. Hold the side rail firmly with a G-cramp. Cut the shoulders on the waste side. Make several cuts within the joint to make chiselling out the waste easier. Remove the waste with a sharp 25 mm firmer chisel, working from both sides. Check the bottom of the joint for flatness and adjust it as required.

4 At the head end square the shoulder lines across the bottom edge. Using a marking gauge set to 10 mm, mark a line on the edge between these set-out lines. Then set the marking gauge to 70 mm and

TOOLS
• Tape or rule and pencil
• Circular saw
• Jigsaw
• Tenon saw
• Power mitre saw
• Combination square
• Marking gauge
• Chisel: 25 mm firmer
• Electric drill
• Drill bits: 4.5 mm, 10 mm, 40 mm Forstner
• Hammer
• Nail punch
• Compasses
• Two G-cramps
• Screwdriver to suit
• Spanner to suit
• Cork sanding block

mark a line between the shoulder lines on the face side (to make a stopped housing 70 mm up from the bottom edge for the head rail). Working carefully, use a tenon saw to cut the shoulders at an angle on the face to the gauge line on the face edge. Make several saw cuts within the joint, taking care not to go past the gauge lines.

This lounger is made from Western red cedar, a durable softwood for exterior use. It is also a lightweight timber, well suited to furniture that is often moved. You can, however, add wheels to the legs at one end if you like.

5 Drill holes into the housing and remove the waste with a sharp chisel, cutting across the grain by striking the chisel straight down on the shoulder lines. Turn the chisel around, hold the ground side down at about 45 degrees and strike it to sever the grain. Turn the chisel ground side up and pare away the waste across the grain from the edge to the end of the housing. Remove a little at a time until the required depth is reached. Ensure the shoulders and the bottom of the joint are straight.

31

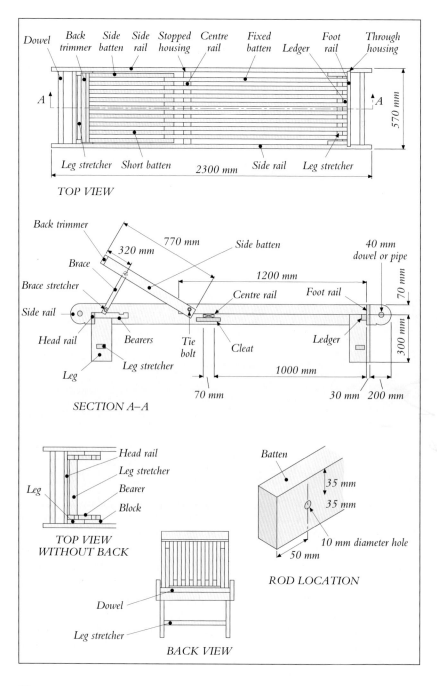

TOP VIEW

SECTION A–A

TOP VIEW
WITHOUT BACK

ROD LOCATION

BACK VIEW

MATERIALS★

Part	Material	Finished length	No.
Side rail	115 x 30 mm Western red cedar	2300 mm	2
Foot rail	115 x 30 mm Western red cedar	530 mm	1
Head/centre rail	70 x 30 mm Westerm red cedar	530 mm	2
Leg	115 x 30 mm Western red cedar	300 mm	4
Leg stretcher	70 x 30 mm Western red cedar	450 mm	2
Ledger	30 x 40 mm Western red cedar	450 mm	1
Fixed batten	70 x 30 mm Western red cedar	1200 mm	8
Short batten	70 x 30 mm Western red cedar	740 mm	7
Side batten	70 x 30 mm Western red cedar	760 mm	2
Back trimmer	70 x 30 mm Western red cedar	505 mm	1
Brace	30 x 30 mm Western red cedar	400 mm	2
Brace stretcher	30 x 30 mm Western red cedar	505 mm	1
Bearer	30 x 40 mm Western red cedar	307 mm	2
Block	30 x 40 mm Western red cedar	200 mm	2

OTHER: Two 540 mm pieces of 40 mm dowelling; abrasive paper: 80 grit; 65 x 2.5 mm galvanised raised-head nails; 50 mm x 8 gauge galvanised chipboard screws; ten 75 mm x 8 gauge galvanised chipboard screws; one 600 x 10 mm galvanised threaded rod with two dome nuts and washers to suit; natural oil or finish of your choice

★All material sizes quoted are planed measurements. For timber types and sizes, see page 37. Finished size: 2300 mm long x 580 mm wide x 350 mm high.

6 Make another stopped housing for the centre rail. Measure 1000 mm from the foot housing, then measure a further 70 mm. Square the lines across the face. Now measure 70 mm down from the top edge and mark the end of the housing between the shoulder lines. Square the lines across the bottom edge and mark a depth of 10 mm. Cut the stopped housing in the same manner as before.

FINISHING THE FRAME COMPONENTS

7 Use a combination square and pencil to mark a 45 degree line from each corner across the inside face of both ends of the side rails. Place the point of a compass at the intersection of these lines and draw the curved end of the rail. Cut the shape with a jigsaw, extending it a little way beyond the centre point. (Refer to

the illustration below.) Smooth the edges with 80 grit abrasive paper wrapped around a sanding block.

8 Dowelling is used at the head and foot of the lounger to create the handles. Drill a hole 20 mm deep at the intersection of the 45 degree lines using a Forstner bit. Choose a bit that matches the diameter of the dowelling so that the hole is the correct size.

9 Cut four legs 300 mm long. Square the ends and, with square and marking gauge, set out a housing in the top corner of each leg, 30 mm in from the edge and 70 mm down from the top (see the diagram opposite). Hold the leg firmly with a G-cramp or vice and cut along the leg with a circular saw to the squared line, then cross-cut with a handsaw to remove the waste. Complete the rip cut with the handsaw.

ASSEMBLY
10 Before starting to assemble the lounger, apply a coat of preservative to all the joints if desired.

11 Cut the foot, head and centre rails. Place one side rail flat on a firm surface with the housing side up. Stand all the cross rails in their housings. Skew a 65 mm nail through each cross rail into the side rail. Place the other side rail flat, housing side up, then turn the assembled section over and stand it in the housings. Cut two 540 mm handles from dowelling. Fit them in the holes drilled at the ends, keeping all the pieces in position. Skew-nail the cross rails to the second side rail as for the first side. Cut two cleats from offcuts and fix them to the side rails beneath the centre rail.

12 Position the legs inside the frame with the head and foot rails sitting in the rebates. Drill two 4.5 mm holes through each leg and 3 mm pilot holes into the side rail. Fix the legs with 50 mm screws. For added strength, position a ledger 70 mm down from the top edge on the inside face of the foot rail. Fix it to the rail with three 50 mm screws. Skew-nail the leg stretchers between the legs.

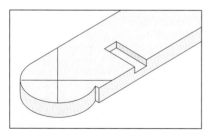

7 *With a compass, draw the curved end of the rail. Cut the shape with a jigsaw, extending past the centre point.*

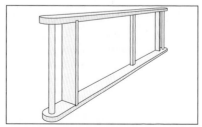

11 *Place the assembled side and cross rails on the second side rail, fit in the handles and nail in the cross rails.*

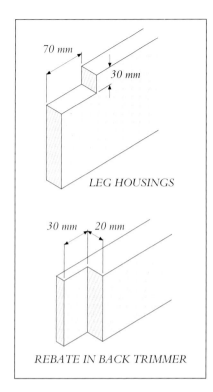

LEG HOUSINGS

REBATE IN BACK TRIMMER

13 Cut the eight fixed battens from 70 x 30 mm timber to the required length, using the mitre saw. Measure 50 mm in from one end on each and square a line across the face. Set a marking gauge to 35 mm and mark the centre of the line. At this set-out point drill a 10 mm hole right through each batten.

14 Lay one batten in position, against the inside of the side rails with the hole at the head end, and bore a corresponding 10 mm hole right through the side rail. Repeat this procedure to drill a hole on the other side rail.

15 Use the offcuts from the battens as spacers. Place the spacers between the side rail and the batten. Push the batten against the spacers, with the end of the batten against the inside of the foot rail. Position all the battens and insert the tie rod to help keep the holes in alignment. Nail through the outside of the foot rail into the end of the batten with two 65 x 2.5 mm galvanised raised-head nails. Nail the other end of the batten from underneath, through the centre rail. Remove the tie rod.

16 Cut the back trimmer 505 mm long from 70 x 30 mm timber. This should allow it to fit between the side rails with a little clearance. To cut a rebate joint to house each side batten, square a line across the face and down each side, 30 mm in from each end. Set a marking gauge to 20 mm and mark a line across the ends and along each side to the squared lines (see the diagram at left). Cut the rebate on the waste side of the line with a circular saw. Remove the waste.

17 Cut seven short battens 740 mm long and two side battens 760 mm long for the adjustable back. Set out and drill a hole at one end of each as for the fixed battens.

INSERTING THE TIE ROD
18 Insert a length of 10 mm threaded rod through the side rail and one 760 mm batten. Continue pushing the rod alternately through a

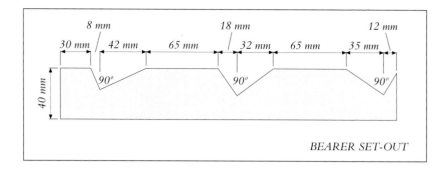

8 mm   18 mm   12 mm

30 mm   42 mm   65 mm   32 mm   65 mm   35 mm

40 mm

90°   90°   90°

BEARER SET-OUT

fixed batten and a short batten, finishing with the remaining 760 mm batten inside the opposite side rail. Place dome nuts and washers on each end of the rod.

19 Position the back trimmer and fix it through each outside batten with three 65 x 2.5 mm galvanised raised-head nails. Use the batten offcuts as spacers and nail through the trimmer into the ends of the battens as before.

20 Cut two braces that will be used to adjust the angle of the back. Measure 30 mm from the end of each piece and drill a 4.5 mm hole in the centre. On the outside batten measure 320 mm from the trimmer

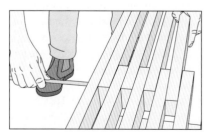

18 Insert the threaded rod through the side rail, through the fixed and short battens and out the other side.

and 30 mm up from the bottom edges. Drill a 4.5 mm hole.

21 Cut two bearers 307 mm long. Notches are cut on the bearers to determine the adjustable angle of the back. Refer to the diagram above and mark the set-out on each bearer. Use a jigsaw to cut the three notches at 90 degree angles.

22 Position the bearers on each side against the leg, taking care to keep the top flush with the top of the leg. Place a timber block of the same thickness as the leg between the bearer and the side rail and fix with three 75 mm x 8 gauge screws.

23 Fix the braces to the back with 75 mm x 8 gauge screws. Cut a 505 mm long stretcher to fit between the braces. Position the stretcher 30 mm up from the bottom of the braces and fix with 50 mm x 8 gauge chipboard screws.

FINISHING
24 Apply the protective finish of your choice to the lounger.

TIMBER

TIMBER CONDITIONS

Timber is sold in three conditions:
- sawn or rough sawn: brought to a specific (nominal) size by band saw
- planed: either planed all round (PAR), planed on two sides (P2S) or double planed (DP)
- moulded: planed to a specific profile for architraves, window sills, skirting boards and so on

Planed timber is sold using the same nominal dimensions as sawn timber, for example 100 x 50 mm, but the surfaces have all been machined down to a flat, even width and thickness so that the '100 x 50 mm' timber becomes 91 x 41 mm when dressed. The chart on the right shows the sizes for seasoned timber in its sawn (nominal) state and after dressing.

Moulded timbers are also ordered by their nominal sizes. Their finished sizes will generally compare with those given in the chart for planed timber, but check them carefully at the timber yard as there will be many variations.

UNSEASONED TIMBER

The sizes for unseasoned timber will vary somewhat as the timber is still in the process of shrinking. This applies particularly for timbers measuring more than 100 x 50 mm. It is possible to have the supplier plane unseasoned timber to the required size.

Sawn (nominal) size (mm)	Size after planing (mm)
25	19
31	23
38	30
50	41
75	66
100	91
125	115
150	138
175	160

TREATED TIMBER

Treated timber is, however, sold in its finished size. Some of the available sizes are:

70 x 35 mm   70 x 45 mm
90 x 45 mm   90 x 90 mm
120 x 45 mm

TIMBER LENGTHS

Timber is now sold in stock lengths, beginning at 1.8 m and increasing by 300 mm to 2.1 m, 2.4 m and so on. Short lengths and offcuts are also usually available.

TIMBER FOR OUTDOOR USE

Garden furniture requires timber able to withstand the elements. Among the possible choices are treated pine, Western red cedar, iroko and other hardwoods. All these timbers will require some type of protective finish. If the timber has an attractive colour or grain, a natural oil finish will enhance its appearance.

The ideal spot to while away your hard-earned leisure, this swing seat is constructed from treated pine and given a clear, natural finish.

Swing seat

The A-frame construction of this appealing garden swing takes up relatively little space, making it suitable for large or small gardens. It is not difficult to make.

MAKING THE FRAME

1 Cut the beam to length using a power mitre saw. Measure 150 mm from each end and square a line around the beam. This is the outside edge of the A-frame.

2 To mark the bevels at each end of the legs, set up a builders square with rafter buttons. Fix one button to the blade of the square at 316 mm and the other on the stock at 97 mm. Place the leg on edge and mark the position of the stock on the timber (see the diagram below). This is the bevel for the foot cut. Then mark the position of the blade on the edge of the timber. Slide the square along the timber, lining up the stock with the previous blade position. Mark the blade length again and slide the square along. Repeat until you have

TOOLS

- Tape or rule and pencil
- Power mitre saw
- Circular saw
- Jigsaw
- Handsaw
- Combination square
- Builders square and rafter buttons
- Sawhorses
- Hand plane
- Marking gauge
- Hammer
- Electric drill
- Drill bits: 4.5 mm, 8 mm, 10 mm
- Screwdriver and spanners
- G-cramps
- Chisel: 25 mm
- Cork sanding block

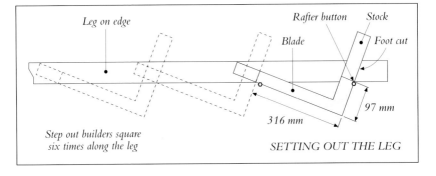

Leg on edge

Rafter button   Stock

Blade   Foot cut

97 mm

316 mm

Step out builders square six times along the leg

SETTING OUT THE LEG

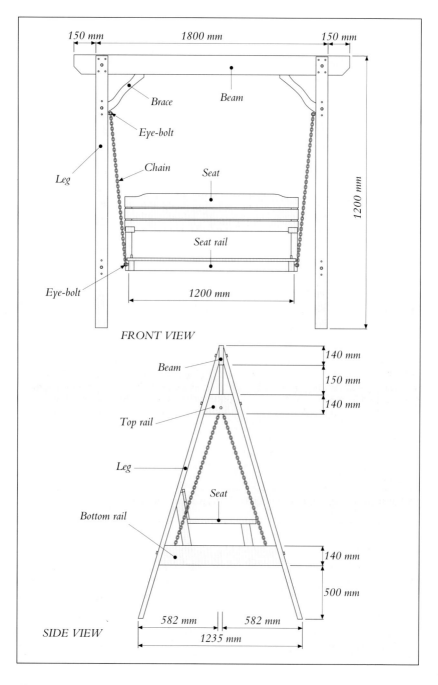

150 mm 1800 mm 150 mm

Brace

Beam

Eye-bolt

Chain Seat

Leg

1200 mm

Seat rail

Eye-bolt

1200 mm

FRONT VIEW

Beam

140 mm

150 mm

Top rail

140 mm

Leg

Seat

Bottom rail

140 mm

500 mm

582 mm 582 mm

SIDE VIEW

1235 mm

MATERIALS★

Part	Material	Finished length	No.
Frame			
Beam	140 x 45 mm treated pine	2100 mm	1
Leg	90 x 45 mm treated pine	1987 mm	4
Bottom rail	140 x 45 mm treated pine	960 mm	2
Top rail	140 x 45 mm treated pine	230 mm	2
Seat			
Bearer	70 x 35 mm treated pine	955 mm	2
Back upright	70 x 35 mm treated pine	600 mm	2
Seat rail	70 x 35 mm treated pine	1200 mm	2
Arm support	70 x 35 mm treated pine	275 mm	2
Arm	70 x 35 mm treated pine	600 mm	2
Seat slat	70 x 25 mm treated pine	1284 mm	8
Back slat	70 x 25 mm treated pine	1300 mm	2
Top slat	90 x 25 mm treated pine	1300 mm	1

OTHER: 65 mm x 8 gauge galvanised chipboard screws; twenty-four 50 mm x 8 gauge galvanised chipboard screws; 38 mm x 8 gauge galvanised chipboard screws; eight 75 mm x 10 gauge galvanised chipboard screws; 40 x 2.5 mm galvanised decking nails; 65 x 2.5 mm galvanised raised-head nails; eight 100 x 8 mm galvanised coach screws and washers; two 125 x 10 mm galvanised round-head bolts and nuts; abrasive paper: 120 grit; two 380 mm long wooden corner braces; six 100 mm galvanised eye-bolts with washers and lock nuts; six 5 mm galvanised snap hooks; 4.4 m of 20 mm galvanised chain; preservative; finish of choice

★ Finished size: 2100 mm wide x 1235 deep and 1900 high.

stepped the length six times. The last blade mark is the cut to go against the beam. Square these positions down each face of the leg; cut on the waste side. This is the leg template.

3 Clamp the timber on edge to the sawhorses and cut with a handsaw. Follow the set-out lines and regularly check both sides of the cut, especially the top cut. If necessary, plane the cut end to even the bevel. To cut the second leg, place the first leg on top of it, edge to edge, and trace the bevels and length from the first leg onto the second leg. Cut to match.

4 Place the two legs on edge with the top ends resting either side of an offcut of beam timber. Move the bottom of the legs 1200 mm apart. Check that the top fits neatly against the offcut, and lay a straight edge against the feet to check the bevel. Adjust as required.

5 Measure 500 mm from the straight edge at the bottom of the legs and place a bottom rail over the legs. On the rail, mark the angle of the legs. On the legs, mark the top and bottom of the rail. Place a top rail across the legs, 150 mm down from the beam, parallel to the first rail. Mark as before. Remove the rails and join the set-out across the face. Cut the rails to length.

6 Check the fit. Use a square to transfer the marks down the inside face of the legs. Use these four pieces as a pattern for the other side frame. Construct it in the same way.

7 Set a gauge to 22 mm and mark a line on the inside face of each leg between the squared lines. Hold each

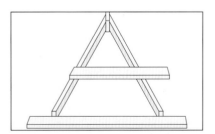

4 Check the fit of the legs against the beam. Place the bottom rail parallel to the bottom edge and mark the angle.

rail on the gauged line, between the squared lines. Nail a 65 x 2.5 mm raised-head nail through the outside of the leg. When all the joints are fitted and the frame has been nailed, drill through the leg with an 8 mm bit down to the centre of the end of each rail. Drill a 4.5 mm pilot hole as deep as possible into the end of the rails. Put a 100 x 8 mm coach screw with washer into the hole and tighten. Repeat at the ends of all rails.

8 Place the frame on the face of one leg. Slide the beam in place at the top of the frame. Line up the outer edge of the frame with the square marks on the beam. Drill a 10 mm hole through the leg, the beam and the other leg. Fix with a 125 x 10 mm round-head nut and bolt. Check the beam is square to the leg. Measure 30 mm up from the bottom of the beam and drill two 4.5 mm holes through the leg. Screw 65 mm screws through the leg, into the beam. Drill two 4.5 mm holes through the leg 30 mm from the top of the beam. Fix with 38 mm screws.

9 Fit the brace between the top rail and the beam. Fix the brace through the rail with a 65 mm screw. To fix the top of the brace to the bottom edge of the beam, drill a 4.5 mm hole near the end of the brace and fit a 38 mm screw into the beam.

CONSTRUCTING THE SEAT

10 Cut two bearers to length using the mitre saw. Square a line across the

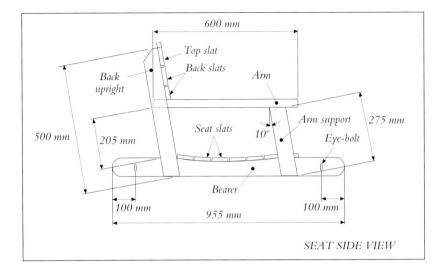

600 mm

Top slat

Back slats

Arm

Back
upright

275 mm

Arm support

10°

Eye-bolt

Seat slats

500 mm

205 mm

Bearer

100 mm

100 mm

955 mm

SEAT SIDE VIEW

top edge, 200 mm from each end. Measure in another 70 mm and square a line as before (see the diagram on page 45). Mark the centre of the bearer and square a line across the top edge and down the faces. Mark 10 mm down the centre line and tack in a small nail. To curve the seat, bend a thin piece of timber over the nail and out to the 70 mm lines. Trace the curve onto the bearer. Clamp the bearer to a sawhorse and cut the curve on the waste side with a jigsaw. Smooth with abrasive paper.

11 Square both 200 mm set-out lines across the inside face and both edges of the bearers. Measure in 35 mm from this and square a line around all sides. Set a gauge to 10 mm and mark both edges between the lines for the rail housings. Clamp the bearers to a sawhorse and cut on the waste side. Clean the joint.

12 Cut two back uprights to length with one end 10 degrees off square. For the halving joint, measure in 72 mm and mark a shoulder line across the face, parallel to the angle cut. Square this line down each edge. Set a marking gauge to 17 mm and mark a line along the edges of the timber and across the end. Make left and right uprights. Clamp the upright flat on a sawhorse and cut the housing on the waste side. Make several cuts across the joint. Remove the waste; level the housing bottom.

13 Cut two arm supports, each end angled at 10 degrees. Set out and cut a housing at the bottom end as for the back uprights (see the diagram above). Cut one left and one right. Cut two seat rails 1200 mm long on the mitre saw. Apply preservative to the housing and the end of the rails. Position the rails in the housing on

43

the side of the bearers. Drill two 4.5 mm holes through the outside of the bearer. Fix the rails with 75 mm x 10 gauge screws. Fix the back uprights and arm supports to the bearers with three 50 mm x 8 gauge screws at the 200 mm set-out lines.

14 Cut two arms. Measure in 70 mm on one end and square a line across the face. Mark a line on the inside edge 10 degrees off square and square a line back across the bottom. Gauge a line 35 mm in from the edge, from the squared line on the face across the end and back to the squared line on the opposite face. Cut out the corner with a handsaw. Round the front end of the arm with a jigsaw. Smooth with 120 grit abrasive paper. To fix the arm, measure 205 mm from the top of the bearer up the back upright. Hold the arm on top of this mark and drill a 4.5 mm hole. Fit two 50 mm x 8 gauge galvanised chipboard screws through the back upright into the centre of the arm. Place another two screws through the top of the arm into the arm support.

ADDING THE SLATS

15 Cut eight seat slats with the mitre saw. The two front slats fit around the arm support. Hold the first slat with the ends flush on the outside face of the arm supports. Mark the position of the inside face of the support on the edge of the slat. Square this line across the face of the slat. The slat overhangs the seat rail by 20 mm. Set a gauge to 20 mm to mark a line parallel to the front edge, from the squared line to the outside edge. Place a cross on the opposite side of the line to indicate the section to be removed. Hold the slat on a sawhorse and, with a handsaw, rip down the grain to the squared line then across the slat on the waste side. Clean the cut with a chisel. Sand the sharp edge with 120 grit abrasive paper and apply preservative to the ends and underneath.

16 Fix the slat to the bearer with two 40 x 2.5 mm decking nails at each end. Evenly space two more nails into the rail. Fit the second slat with a 15 mm cut-out in the front edge to fit the back of the support.

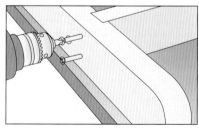

13 Fit the rails in the housings on the side of the bearers and fix them with two 75 mm screws.

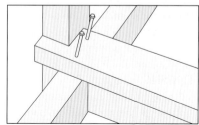

15 Fit the first slat around the arm support so that it overhangs the seat rail by 20 mm.

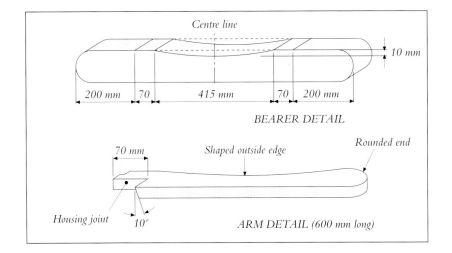

Centre line

10 mm

200 mm | 70 | 415 mm | 70 | 200 mm

BEARER DETAIL

70 mm | *Shaped outside edge* | *Rounded end*

Housing joint | 10°

ARM DETAIL (600 mm long)

Leave a 5 mm gap between the slats. Nail the other slats to the bearers, overhanging 17 mm each end and with 5 mm between. Set out and cut the last seat slats to fit the upright.

17 Cut the top slat to length. Square a line 100 mm from each end. Gauge a line 70 mm in from the edge to the squared line. Use a can or jar to draw an inside and outside curve. Cut on the jigsaw. Place the slat on the back uprights, overhanging the top and ends by 5 mm. Fix with 40 x 2.5 mm decking nails. Cut and fix the second and third slats with a 5 mm gap between. Fit the third slat around the arms as before.

FINISHING
18 On the bearers measure 35 mm from the top edge and 100 mm from each end. Drill an 8 mm hole through the bearer and place a 100 mm eye-bolt through each hole.

Secure it with a washer and lock nut, with the eye square to the bearer. On the frame measure 100 mm up from the bottom of the top rail and drill an 8 mm hole through rail and brace. Place a 100 mm eye-bolt through the hole and secure it with washer and lock nut. Cut four 1100 mm lengths of chain. Attach the chain to the eye-bolts with a 5 mm snap hook.

19 Apply a suitable outdoor finish of your choice to the project to protect the timber from the weather.

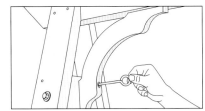

18 Drill a hole through both the brace and rail. Insert an eye-bolt and secure with a washer and nut.

Arbour seat

The lattice sides and roof of this sturdy arbour seat provide shelter from the sun while still letting through breezes to keep you cool. The construction is straightforward and does not require special skill.

PREPARING THE POSTS AND RAILS

1 Cut the four corner posts to length with a circular saw. Place the posts side by side with the ends flush and measure 350 mm from the bottom, then a further 90 mm. Use a builders square to transfer these marks across all the posts. Mark a cross between the set-out lines to represent the housing for the bottom rails. Select two back posts and square the set-out onto a second side of each. Remember, you will need one left-hand and one right-hand post. For the side intermediate rail housing, measure up 1000 mm from the top of the bottom rail housing then a further 90 mm, square the lines and mark with a cross as before (see the top diagram on page 48). Set a gauge and mark a line 10 mm in from the edge between each shoulder line.

2 Clamp one back post firmly on the sawhorses. Set the circular saw to cut 10 mm deep. Line up the notch in the base plate of the saw with the squared lines and slowly cut a through housing (cutting on the waste side of the set-out). Make several other cuts in the housing to

TOOLS
• Tape measure and pencil
• Circular saw
• Handsaw
• Builders square
• Marking gauge
• Chisel: 25 mm
• Electric drill
• Drill bit: 4.5 mm
• Sash cramps
• Screwdriver
• Hammer
• Rafter buttons
• Sawhorses

make it easier to remove the waste timber, and clean the bottom of the housing with a 25 mm chisel. Take care not to go past the gauged lines. Use an offcut of rail material to check the bottom of each housing for flatness and width. Cut the remaining housings in the back posts in the same way, and then cut the housings in the front posts.

3 Cut the side bottom and intermediate rails and the back bottom rail to length.

An asset to any garden, this arbour seat is constructed in treated pine and then given a protective coating of clear decking oil for a long life of year-round use.

4 Cut two side top rails. To enable these two rails to overhang the posts, measure 150 mm and then a further 90 mm from each end, and square lines at these points across the face and approximately 10 mm down each edge. Gauge a line 10 mm deep and cut the housings for the post. Determine the front and back of the rail. Square the set-out lines of the rear housing across the inside edge and opposite face of each rail. Set a marking gauge to 30 mm and mark a line between these set-out lines and in the bottom of the housing (see the diagram below). You will need a left-hand and a right-hand rail. Hold the timber on edge and cut down the set-out lines of the housing with a handsaw to the gauge lines. Remove the waste as before.

5 Cut the back top rail to length. Square a line across the face and down each side 30 mm from each end. Set a marking gauge to 10 mm and mark a line from the squared line along the edge and across the end. Cut and clean the housings.

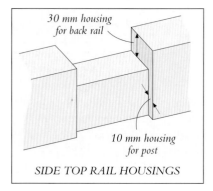

SIDE TOP RAIL HOUSINGS

30 mm housing for back rail

10 mm housing for post

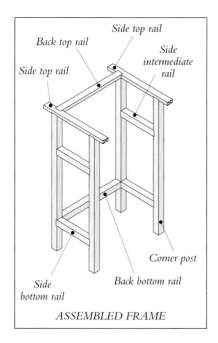

Back top rail

Side top rail

Side top rail

Side intermediate rail

Corner post

Side bottom rail

Back bottom rail

ASSEMBLED FRAME

ASSEMBLING THE FRAME

6 Apply preservative to all joints. Place the posts on a flat surface and position the side bottom rails one at a time in the housings with the outside faces flush. Drill two 4.5 mm holes at an angle through the bottom face of the rail. Hold the rail in the housing at 90 degrees to the post and fix it in place with two 65 mm screws. Additional screws placed through the top will add strength to the joint. Position the side intermediate rails and fix them as before. Take care to keep the frame as close as possible to square while you are assembling it. If you have sash cramps, place them over the frame to pull the joints tight. Place the top rail over the ends of the posts (ensure you have one left-hand

MATERIALS★

PART	MATERIAL	FINISHED LENGTH	NO.
Corner post	90 x 90 mm treated pine	2100 mm	4
Side rail	90 x 90 mm treated pine	620 mm	4
Back bottom rail	90 x 90 mm treated pine	1220 mm	1
Side top rail	90 x 45 mm treated pine	1080 mm	2
Back top rail	90 x 45 mm treated pine	1260 mm	1
Rafter	90 x 45 mm treated pine	925 mm	6
Trimmer	90 x 45 mm treated pine	423 mm	4
Seat trimmer	90 x 45 mm treated pine	480 mm	1
Seat front rail	90 x 35 mm treated pine	1200 mm	1
Seat centre upright	90 x 40 mm treated pine	700 mm	1
Seat back upright	40 x 40 mm treated pine	700 mm	2
Seat top rail	40 x 40 mm treated pine	1200 mm	1
Cleats	40 x 40 mm treated pine	to fit	2
Ridge	140 x 35 mm treated pine	1080 mm	1
Arch	140 x 45 mm treated pine	1200 mm	1
Seat/back slats	90 x 20 mm treated pine	1200 mm	12

OTHER: 65 mm x 8 gauge galvanised chipboard screws; 25 mm x 2 mm galvanised raised-head nails; 40 x 2.5 mm twisted-shank decking nails; two 75 mm nail plates; four metal joint connectors; lattice: one sheet 1800 x 1200 mm and one sheet 2400 x 1200 mm; about 50 m of 18 x 12 mm beading; abrasive paper: 80 grit; ready-made finial; preservative; finish of choice

★ Finished size: 1380 mm wide x 1080 mm deep x 2450 mm high.

and one right-hand frame) and drill four 4.5 mm holes through the face into the top of each post. Secure with 65 mm screws.

7 You may require a helping hand for the next step. Stand each side frame on its front edge and position the two back rails in the housings. The top rail is screwed through the top face into the ends of the post with 65 mm screws. Fix a nail plate over the top of each joint. The bottom rail has four screws skewed into the post as before. If necessary, nail a temporary brace over the front side to keep the frame steady and parallel while you work.

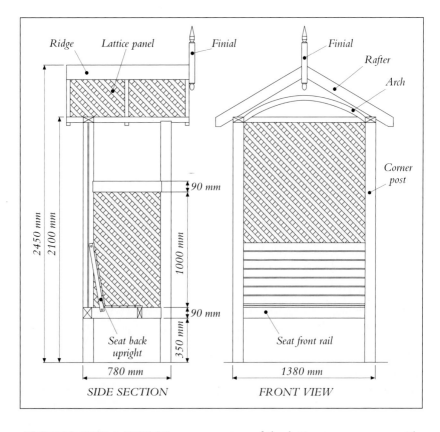

Ridge Lattice panel Finial Finial

Rafter

Arch

2450 mm

2100 mm

90 mm

1000 mm

90 mm

Corner post

Seat back
upright

350 mm

780 mm

Seat front rail

1380 mm

SIDE SECTION

FRONT VIEW

ADDING THE LATTICE

8 To determine the size of the lattice panel, measure the inside of the frame and reduce the measurement by 3 mm on all sides for clearance. Mark the required measurements on the face of the lattice and place a straight piece of timber on each mark. Draw a line the length of the cut along the straight edge. Place two 100 x 50 mm lengths of timber on a flat, firm surface. Position the lattice on top of the timber with the cutting line between the timbers. Nail or clamp the straight piece of timber on

top of the lattice to serve as a guide for a circular saw. Check the blade will line up with the marked line and cut the lattice, taking care to keep the base plate against the straight edge and to support the offcut.

9 The lattice panels are beaded into the frame. Gauge a line 20 mm in from the back around the back opening. Cut the 18 x 12 mm bead to fit around all sides of the opening and fix it on the gauged line with 25 x 2 mm galvanised raised-head nails. Place the lattice in the frame

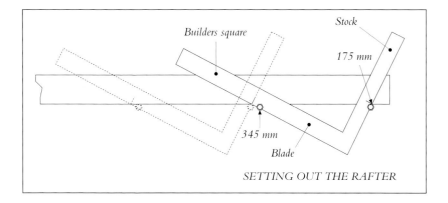

Builders square

Stock

175 mm

345 mm

Blade

SETTING OUT THE RAFTER

and secure it in position by cutting and nailing another layer of beading around the opening on the other side of the lattice. Repeat the process for the side panels.

CONSTRUCTING
THE ROOF

10 Set up a builders steel square with a pair of rafter buttons attached. Set the button on the blade to 345 mm (span) and that on the stock to 175 mm (rise). Place the square on a piece of rafter timber and pencil in the angle of the stock at the top (see the diagram above). Mark the position of the blade button. Slide the square along the rafter and line up the stock with the mark. Mark the blade button point for a second time and slide the square along once again to line up the stock with this point. Mark the line of the stock at this location. This line will represent the edge of the bird's-mouth housing. Measure 25 mm up this line and slide the square along the rafter to line the blade up with this mark and mark the

line of the blade. Measure out 150 mm along the blade from the line. Slide the square along the rafter and mark yet another line along the stock at the point. This is the bottom cut of the rafter.

11 The line for the top cut now needs to be repositioned by half the thickness of the ridge (17 mm) before it is cut. Position the square at the top of the rafter and slide down 17 mm. Cut the rafter to shape. Use a circular saw for each end and a handsaw for the bird's-mouth cuts. Take care with the cutting of this rafter, as it will be used as a template for all the rafters.

12 Place the template rafter on another piece of timber. Trace around the template and cut a second rafter to match. Place these two rafters in position with a piece of ridge material in between to test your set-out. Adjust as required. Place the template rafter on top of the other rafter material (three for each side).

Use a square to transfer the set-out onto the remaining rafters and cut as before.

13 Cut the ridge to the same length as the side top rails. Set a marking gauge to 20 mm and mark a line on the faces parallel to the top edge. Find the centre of the ridge. Place a rafter against the centre and mark the position, squaring the lines around to the opposite side. Place the ridge on one side top rail with the ends flush. Mark the front end so the set-out will be accurate. Transfer the centre rafter position onto the side rail. Repeat for the other side.

14 Place the first rafter on a flat surface. Stand the ridge on end and align the top edge of the rafter with the gauged line. Drill two 4.5 mm holes through the ridge. Fix the ridge to the end of the rafter with two 65 mm x 8 gauge screws. Fix the other rafters on this side to the ridge with two screws in each, ensuring they line up with the gauge line and the end one is flush with the ridge. Hold the opposite rafters in position

and drill a 4.5 mm hole through the top edge. A 65 mm x 8 gauge screw is used to fix each to the ridge. Drill another screw hole through the other side of the ridge at an angle to hold the lower edge of the rafter.

15 Lift the assembled roof frame into position. Check the outside rafters are flush on the ends and the centre rafter lines up with the previous set-out. Fix the frame in place through the top rails with 65 mm x 8 gauge screws. Cut a trimmer to fit between each rafter. Fix each trimmer with two screws, 30 mm from each end of the rafter and square to the top edge. Cut and bead in a lattice panel between each rafter in the same manner as for the sides and back.

FITTING THE SEAT

16 Cut two back uprights and one top rail for the seat. Square each end. Measure 100 mm from the back on the top of the side bottom rail and mark with a pencil on the inside edge. Hold the upright with the back edge on the 100 mm mark and the top end over the lattice beading on the corner post.

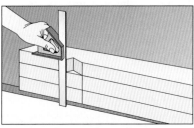

12 Place the template rafter on top of the other rafter material. Use a square to transfer the bird's-mouth set-out.

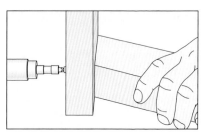

14 Place the first rafter on a flat surface. Stand the ridge on end and align the rafter with the gauged line.

Trace around the top on the beading. Cut the beading away with a sharp chisel so the upright sits flat against the post. Repeat on the other side. Fix the seat top rail to the top of each upright with the end flush, using one 65 mm x 8 gauge screw in each. Fix the assembled section in place with the top into the bead and the bottom aligned with the 100 mm mark.

17 Cut the seat front rail to length and fix it in place with a metal joint connector 480 mm in from the back posts. Cut a seat trimmer, fit it between the front and back rail, and secure it with screws. Add a joint connector to each end for extra strength. Fix the centre upright to the side of the trimmer and under the top rail. Cut two seat cleats to fit between the back upright and the front rail. Screw flush with the top edge of the side rail.

18 Cut twelve slats for the back and seat. Fix the back slats first with 40 x 2.5 mm twisted-shank nails, allowing a 3 mm gap between each board. Start at the bottom and work towards the top,

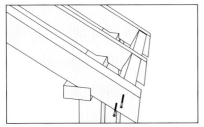

15 Fit a trimmer between each rafter. Check that the trimmers are square to the top edge, then fix in place.

keeping the ends flush with the uprights. Use two nails in each slat. Check periodically for parallel. Fix the seat slats in the same manner. The last board overhangs the front rail.

FINISHING

19 Measure the opening between the side top rails. Cut the piece of timber for the arch to fit between them. Square a line at the centre. On each end, measure up the thickness of the top side rails (45 mm) and tack a nail at this point. Tack another nail at the top of the centre line.

20 Bend a piece of beading around the three nails and trace on the inside of the curve. At the centre line measure down 45 mm and tack in another nail. Bend the beading around this nail and down to the bottom corners of the timber to make a parallel curve. Cut the curve on the waste side of the line with a jigsaw. Sand smooth with 80 grit abrasive paper.

21 Fix the arch in place with a 65 mm x 8 gauge screw through the bottom of the arch into the edge of the rail. A second screw should be skewed through the back to prevent the arch twisting around.

22 As a finishing touch, screw a ready-made finial to the top of the roof through the back of the rafters.

23 Complete the arbour seat by applying your chosen finish.

Designed on traditional lines to furnish your outdoor living area with style, this comfortable chair is constructed in sapele with a natural oil finish.

Traditional garden chair

This project for experienced woodworkers is sturdily constructed with mortise and tenon joints. The traditional styling suits any setting, and the seat is slightly curved for comfort.

CONSTRUCTING THE FRAME

1 Cut two back legs using a power mitre saw. Select and mark the face side and face edge. On one leg measure up 340 mm from one end and square a pencil mark across the face side and edge to represent the bottom of the side rail mortise (see the diagram on page 56). Mark the side rail height (66 mm) up from this and square a pencil line on the face side and edge. Set a mortise gauge to mark a 12 mm wide mortise 14 mm in from the face edge between these two set-out lines. Measure up a further 200 mm and then an additional 50 mm for the arm. Set out a mortise (12 x 50 mm) for the arm. Repeat this set-out for the second leg.

2 Cut two front legs. Select and mark the face side and face edge and cut the bottom end square. Place a back leg flat on the bench, face side up. Place a front leg on top, face side down, with the bottom ends and face edges flush. Use a square to transfer the side rail mortise position onto the face edge of the front leg. Use the mortise gauge to complete the set-out. Repeat for the other leg.

(see the diagram on page 56)

TOOLS

- Measuring tape and pencil
- Power mitre saw
- Jigsaw
- Tenon saw
- Mortise gauge
- Marking gauge
- Combination square
- Router with 3 mm rounding and 18 mm straight bit
- Electric drill
- Drill bits: 3 mm, 4.5 mm, 10 mm, countersink bits
- Two G-cramps
- Chisels: 12 mm mortise, 25 mm firmer
- Hand plane
- Builders square
- Hammer and nail punch
- Three sash cramps
- Screwdriver to suit

3 Using a pencil, mark the top of the back leg 200 mm above the arm mortise and square a line around the timber. Set a marking gauge to mark a line 66 mm from the front edge on the face side, and draw a line to the top of the side rail mortise. Draw a straight line from this intersection to

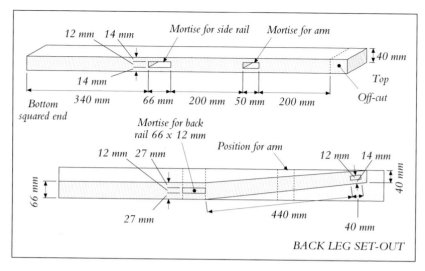

12 mm   14 mm   Mortise for side rail   Mortise for arm

40 mm

14 mm

Top

Bottom squared end   340 mm   66 mm   200 mm   50 mm   200 mm   Off-cut

Mortise for back rail 66 x 12 mm

Position for arm

12 mm   27 mm

12 mm   14 mm

66 mm

40 mm

27 mm   440 mm   40 mm

BACK LEG SET-OUT

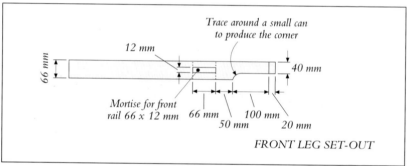

Trace around a small can to produce the corner

12 mm

66 mm

40 mm

Mortise for front rail 66 x 12 mm   66 mm   100 mm

50 mm   20 mm

FRONT LEG SET-OUT

the square top line at the back edge of the timber. Measure and mark 40 mm in from the back edge at the top. Place a rule from the 40 mm mark to the top of the side rail mortise on the front edge of the timber. Mark with a pencil.

4 To remove the bulk of the waste from the mortises, use an electric drill with a 10 mm bit. Place masking tape around the bit to indicate the depth to be bored (40 mm). Hold the

timber over a solid point of the bench using a G-cramp or vice. Cut

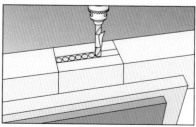

4 Drill out the bulk of the waste from the mortises, using masking tape on the bit to indicate the depth.

MATERIALS★

Part	Material	Finished length	No.
Back leg	90 x 40 mm sapele	900 mm	2
Front leg	66 x 40 mm sapele	580 mm	2
Side rail	66 x 40 mm sapele	510 mm	2
Front/back rail	66 x 40 mm sapele	560 mm	2
Top rail	66 x 30 mm sapele	560 mm	1
Arm	140 x 40 mm sapele	600 mm	2
Back slat	66 x 18 mm sapele	455 mm	4
Back slat (centre)	90 x 18 mm sapele	455 mm	1
Seat slat	66 x 18 mm sapele	600 mm	6
Seat slat (short)	66 x 18 mm sapele	520 mm	1
Cleat	35 x 20 mm sapele	484 mm	2

OTHER: 25 mm x 1.5 mm galvanised raised-head nails; 30 mm x 8 gauge galvanised countersunk screws; ten 50 mm x 8 gauge galvanised countersunk screws; abrasive paper: 120 grit; epoxy adhesive; preservative; finish of choice

★ All material sizes quoted are planed measurements. For timber types and sizes, see page 37. Finished size: 600 mm wide x 620 mm deep x 850 mm high.

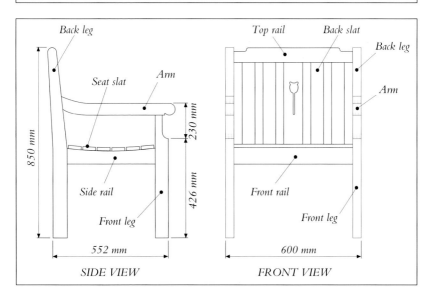

SIDE VIEW   FRONT VIEW

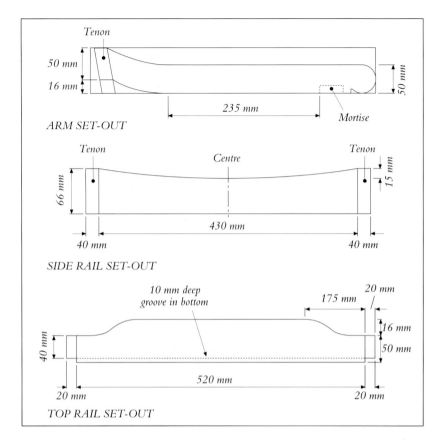

Tenon

50 mm

16 mm

235 mm

50 mm

Mortise

ARM SET-OUT

Tenon

Centre

Tenon

66 mm

15 mm

430 mm

40 mm

40 mm

SIDE RAIL SET-OUT

10 mm deep
groove in bottom

175 mm

20 mm

40 mm

16 mm

50 mm

520 mm

20 mm

20 mm

TOP RAIL SET-OUT

away the remaining waste with a 12 mm mortise chisel to finish 40 mm deep. Trim the mortise sides with a 25 mm firmer chisel. Take care chiselling out the mortise: hold the chisel upright so the recess is straight and true to size.

5 Clamp the back leg flat on a solid surface, with the cutting line on the face side overhanging the edge. Place the jigsaw on the surface and hold it firmly. Cut slowly along the line on the waste side. Take it easy, as the timber is thick and the saw may jump. Use a new, sharp blade for the best result. Place the cut leg on edge

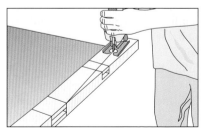

5 Shape the back leg by cutting along the set-out using a jigsaw held firmly to prevent it jumping.

in a vice and true up the edges with a hand plane. Check the face side is square. Round over the tops of the legs with abrasive paper.

6 For the top rail mortise, measure up the face edge of the back leg 440 mm from the back rail mortise. Then measure up 40 mm (the length of the mortise) and square a line across the face side at these points. Set the mortise gauge to mark a 12 mm wide mortise, 14 mm in from the front edge. Repeat for the other leg, remembering you need one left-hand and one right-hand leg. Drill and chisel the mortise 20 mm deep.

7 To shape the front legs, measure up 50 mm from the top of the side rails and square a pencil line around the leg. Measure 40 mm in from the back edge on this line. Pencil a parallel line from this mark to the top of the leg. With a small can or jar, trace a curve between the parallel line and the front edge of the leg. Cut the curve with a jigsaw. Clean up the edge with abrasive paper.

8 On the front leg measure 150 mm up from the top edge of the side rail mortise and square a shoulder line right around the leg. This will leave 20 mm above the line for a tenon. Set the mortise gauge as for the side rail (12 mm wide and 14 mm in from the edge) and mark from the shoulder line on the face edge, up across the end and down to the other shoulder line.

9 Hold the leg upright in a vice and, with a tenon saw, cut down both sides of the tenon on the waste side to the squared shoulder lines. Place the leg flat on the bench. Hold it firmly with a cramp or bench hook and cut across the shoulder lines to remove the waste.

10 Using the mitre saw, cut the side rails 510 mm long. Measure in 40 mm from each end and square a shoulder line all around the timber. Mark the tenons 12 mm wide out from these shoulders and around the end. Hold the rails upright in a vice and cut as before. Check for fit in the legs and adjust by paring a little at a time away from the face of the tenons. Take care to remove any waste from the correct side to ensure the faces remain flush.

MAKING THE ARMS

11 Position the legs on the side rail and secure with a sash cramp. Use a

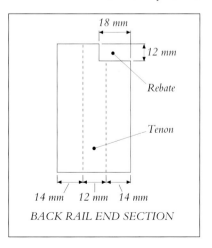

BACK RAIL END SECTION

builders square to check each leg is square to the side rail. Cut the arms to length and hold one under the leg frame with the top edge in line with the top of the arm mortise in the back leg. Place the arm about 20 mm past the face edge of the back leg to allow the tenon to fit into the mortise in the back leg. The bottom edge should be in line with the shoulder of the front leg tenon. Trace around the tenon at the front and mark the shoulder line at the back. Square the tenon tracing around the bottom edge of the arm, and use the mortise gauge to set out the mortise. Drill out and cut the mortise 20 mm deep.

12 The tenon at the back of the arm has a bevelled shoulder to correspond to the slope on the back leg (see the diagram on page 57). Square the marked shoulder line across each edge with a pencil. Turn the arm over and use a rule to line up each squared line and mark the shoulder with a pencil. Use the mortise gauge to mark the tenon and cut it as before. Reposition the arm under the legs and mark the width of the tenon on the face side of the arm.

13 Place the arm flat on the bench. Measure 235 mm from the front mortise along the lower edge and mark across the face side and down the lower edge. Place a thin piece of timber from this point to the bottom of the tenon and mark the curved line with a pencil. Cut the curve with a jigsaw. Mark a parallel line

---

USING A ROUTER

- Read the manufacturer's instructions before operating.
- Always secure the work with cramps or a vice, leaving both hands free to operate the router.
- Wear safety glasses, hearing protection and a dust mask when operating the router.
- Use a scrap of timber to test the router setting before cutting into your project.

---

50 mm up from the lower edge to the squared line. Continue marking parallel to the curved line up to the top of the tenon. Round over and shape the front end of the arm with a jigsaw and abrasive paper.

14 The side rail has a slight curve in the top edge, 15 mm deep in the centre, sloping up to each end. Use a thin piece of timber and a pencil to shape the curve. Cut with a jigsaw.

15 Cut the three rails. Cut a 20 mm tenon either end of each rail, with 9 mm shoulders for the top rail and 14 mm for the front and back rails. To curve the upper edge of the top rail, fix nails 50 mm up from the lower edge and 175 mm in from each shoulder. Use a thin piece of timber and pencil to create the curve and cut along it with a jigsaw. Sand with 120 grit abrasive paper. Place a 3 mm pencil rounding bit in a router and run a small round along the top of

the rail. Router a groove 10 mm deep and 18 mm wide in the lower edge for the back slats.

16 To reduce the top rail tenon from 50 mm to 40 mm, place an 18 mm straight bit in the router. Set the fence on the base so the cutter will run in the centre of the rail, 6 mm in from the edge. Hold the rail firmly upside down in a vice and run the router from left to right with the fence held against the face of the rail.

17 Place the back rail in the vice and adjust the router to cut a rebate in the top edge 12 mm deep and 18 mm wide. Check the fit of all the joints, adjusting as required. At the end of the tenons, cut a mitre with the long face towards the outside.

ASSEMBLING THE CHAIR

18 Assemble each side frame in sash cramps without adhesive. Place a scrap block between the job and the cramps to prevent marking the timber. Adjust it as necessary. Remove any marks by sanding with 120 grit abrasive paper.

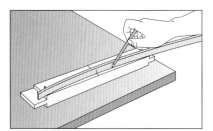

15 Place a piece of timber against the nails at the shoulders and 50 mm up from the centre, and draw the curve.

The centre slat can be decorated with your own cut-out design, or a ready-made baluster can be purchased.

19 Use a small brush or stick to apply epoxy adhesive to the joints, taking care to follow the directions provided. Coat the sides of the tenons and shoulder with the adhesive and smear a little around the inside of the mortise before bringing the joint together. Assemble the frame with two sash cramps underneath, closing up the side rail joint and the arm joint. Use another cramp over the top of the front leg to close the joint under the arm. Place a builders square on each leg and side rail to check for square. Adjust as required. Sight across the job to ensure there is no twist. If necessary, adjust the cramps to correct this. Additional weights or cramps placed on top of the frame can also help. Remove any excess adhesive. When the adhesive has dried, remove the frame from the cramps and use a hand plane to make the surface of the joints flush. Sand the face with 120 grit abrasive paper.

20 Check the remaining rails for fit, with the back rail rebate on the top inside edge. Once satisfied, apply the adhesive and place the sash cramps across the chair parallel to the rails. Lay a builders square inside the frame to check for square. Also check under the leg, between the front and back rails. Remove any excess adhesive. Once the adhesive has dried, remove the cramps and sand the frame to remove any adhesive or pencil marks.

FIXING THE SLATS

21 Cut four back slats to fit between the groove in the top rail and the rebate in the back rail. Cut a wider slat for the centre and cut out a design in the centre. Turn the chair over and position each slat. Maintain a 28 mm space between each slat. Hammer two 25 mm nails through the back of the slat into the top rail groove. Fix the slats into the back rail rebate with two screws measuring 30mm.

22 Cut two cleats to fit between the front and back rails. Hold one in position against the inside of the side

rail, and trace the curved shape of the side rail onto the face of the cleat. Cut the curve with a jigsaw and fix the cleat with four 30 mm screws. Repeat for the second cleat.

23 Cut the seat slats. Position them with the short slat between the front legs, to check the accuracy of the fit. The 600 mm slats overhang each side by 3 mm. Working from the back rail, fix them to the cleats from underneath with two 30 mm screws at each end. Use a nail to keep an even gap between each slat. Round over the front edge of the short slat. Position the front slat between the front legs and counter-bore from underneath the front rail. Fix with two 50 mm screws.

24 Strengthen the corners with scrap timber blocks approximately 150 mm long. Cut each end at 45 degrees to fit against the rail. Fix with a 50 mm screw at each end.

25 Sand out any marks and apply a protective finish so that the chair can be left outside if desired.

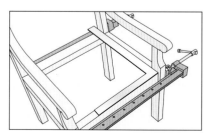

20 Assemble the chair frame, apply adhesive and fit sash cramps parallel to the rails. Check for square.

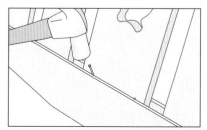

21 Hammer two 25 x 1.5 mm raised-head galvanised nails through the back of the slat into the top rail groove.

Tools for making garden furniture

Some of the most useful tools for making garden furniture are shown below. Build up your tool kit gradually – most of the tools can be purchased from your local hardware store.

SMOOTHING PLANE
Used to smooth the surface of timber before sanding

NAIL PUNCH
Small metal tool used with a hammer for driving a nail head below the surface

ELECTRIC DRILL
Power-driven drill with a variety of bits

CIRCULAR SAW
Power saw for making straight cuts through timber, masonry or metal

MEASURING TAPE
Spring-loaded, flexible steel blade marked in metric units of measure

JIGSAW   Small electric saw with thin blade for cutting curves

G-CRAMP
Holds work firmly to a surface

SASH CRAMP   Long adjustable cramp with screw tension at one end and adjustable sliding stop

BUILDERS SQUARE
Flat, right-angled device for determining 90 degree angles

SPIRIT LEVEL
Used to test work for level (horizontal) and plumb (vertical)

ROUTER   Used for hollowing out or cutting grooves in timber

CLAW HAMMER
Hammer with a round head for driving nails and a split claw for removing them

CHISEL   Used to cut grooves or housings in timber

Index

A
adjustable lounger, 30–6
A-frame construction, 38–42
arbour seat, 46–53

B
backrest, adjustable, 34–6
barbecue table and bench, 16–23
bench, 21–3
bird's-mouth housing, 51–2

C– D
chair
    fold-up, 6, 11–16
    traditional, 54–62
circular seat, 24–9
curves, shaping, 11, 33, 34, 53
dowelled joint, 16

E– F
equipment, 5

finial, 48, 53
fold-up table and chair, 6–16

H
halving joints, 25, 27
housings,
    stopped, 30–31, 33
    through, 30

L– P
lattice
    attaching, 50–1
    cutting, 50
lounger, 30–6
materials, choosing, 4, 37
mortises, removing waste, 56–7
outdoors, timber for, 4, 37
pitch board, 20–1

R– S
rafter buttons, 39, 51, 53
roof construction, 51–2

router
    cutting groove, 13
    using, 60
safety, 5
spacer, using a nail as, 8, 29
swing seat, 38–45

T– W
tables
    fold-up, 6–11
    large, 16–21
tenon
    cutting, 59, 60, 61
tie-rod fitting, 35–6
timber
    conditions, 37
    sizes, 37
    treated, 37
    unseasoned, 37
tree seat, 24–9
work area, 5